W9-AUG-903

I Love Sports

Skateboarding

by Erica Donner

Bullfrog Books

Ideas for Parents and Teachers

Bullfrog Books let children practice reading informational text at the earliest reading levels. Repetition, familiar words, and photo labels support early readers.

Before Reading

- Discuss the cover photo. What does it tell them?

- Look at the picture glossary together. Read and discuss the words.

Read the Book

- "Walk" through the book and look at the photos. Let the child ask questions. Point out the photo labels.

- Read the book to the child, or have him or her read independently.

After Reading

- Prompt the child to think more. Ask: Have you ever been on a skateboard? Did you skate on the street or at a skate park?

Bullfrog Books are published by Jump!
5357 Penn Avenue South
Minneapolis, MN 55419
www.jumplibrary.com

Library of Congress Cataloging-in-Publication Data

Names: Donner, Erica, author.
Title: Skateboarding / by Erica Donner.
Description: Minneapolis, MN: Jump!, Inc. [2017]
Series: I love sports | Includes index.
Identifiers: LCCN 2016007177 (print)
LCCN 2016007542 (ebook)
ISBN 9781620313619 (hardcover: alk. paper)
ISBN 9781624964084 (ebook)
Subjects: LCSH: Skateboarding—Juvenile literature.
Classification: LCC GV859.8 .D65 2017 (print)
LCC GV859.8 (ebook) | DDC 796.22—dc23
LC record available at http://lccn.loc.gov/2016007177

Editor: Kirsten Chang
Series Designer: Ellen Huber
Book Designer: Molly Ballanger
Photo Researcher: Molly Ballanger

Photo Credits: All photos by Shutterstock except: Age Fotostock, 16–17; Getty, 10–11, 12–13, 14–15, 18, 23tl; homydesign/Shutterstock.com, 19; iStock, 4; Rik Jones/Flickr, 8–9; Superstock, 20–21; Thinkstock, 5, 22.

Printed in the United States of America at Corporate Graphics in North Mankato, Minnesota.

Table of Contents

Let's Skate!

Put on your helmet.
Grab your pads.

Let's skate!

Jon sets out cones.
He weaves
between them.

deck

He puts down a rail.

He pops the board up.

The deck slides along the rail.

Mae is at the skate park.

She does tricks.

Ivy is in the bowl.

She goes fast.

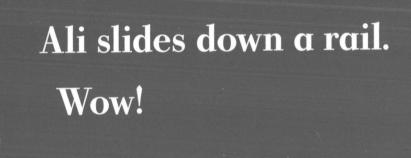

Ali slides down a rail.

Wow!

Bo is in a competition.

He drops into the bowl.

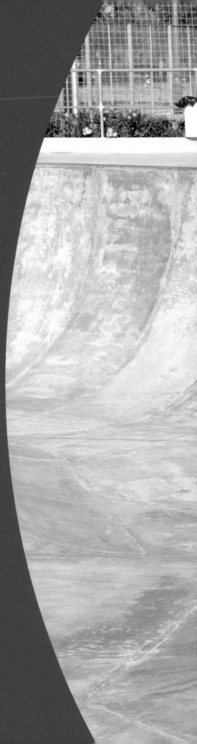

He does tricks.

He flips.

He spins.

There is a half pipe.
Bo gets air. Wow!

Judges were watching.
They gave Bo the highest score.
He wins!

Do you want to try?

Grab your gear.

Let's skate!

At the Skate Park

quarter pipe

ramp

rail

skate bench

Picture Glossary

bowl
A bowl-shaped, smooth concrete surface on which to skate.

half pipe
A U-shaped ramp.

deck
The flat, top part of a skateboard.

weave
To move back and forth or from side to side.

Index

To Learn More

Learning more is as easy as 1, 2, 3.

1) Go to www.factsurfer.com

2) Enter "skateboarding" into the search box.

3) Click the "Surf" button to see a list of websites.

With factsurfer.com, finding more information is just a click away.